CHESHUNT'S PAST
IN PICTURES

CHESHUNT'S PAST IN PICTURES

by

Peter Rooke

The Rockingham Press

First published 1994
by The Rockingham Press
11 Musley Lane,
Ware, Herts SG12 7EN

**A catalogue record for this book is available
from the British Library**

ISBN 1 873468 27 X

Printed in Great Britain by
Biddles Limited
Guildford

Contents

ACKNOWLEDGEMENTS

I have been interested in the history of my native parish since I was a schoolboy, and began collecting pictures of it over forty years ago. In my studies I have been greatly helped and encouraged by Mr Jack Edwards who, when Librarian of Cheshunt, built up a fine local history collection. I have unashamedly used Mr Edwards' own books on Cheshunt as a quarry for information in compiling the present book.

Some pictures have been entrusted to me on loan for this project and I am most grateful to the following: Mr Jon Simons and Miss Jackie Green at Cheshunt library; Mr Tony Stevenson of the Lea Valley Growers Association; Mr John Fishpool of the Waltham Cross store; Mr Tony Blanche of Ripley's the butchers; Mr Jack Edwards, Mr David Dent, and Mr Brian Hewitt.

The following have kindly allowed me to reproduce pictures of which they hold the copyright: the National Portrait Gallery, the B.B.C., Country Life, England Today, Hertfordshire County Record Office, Hertfordshire Publications, The Times, Hertfordshire Mercury, Carleton Photographic, Mr David Fairhurst and Premier Bioscope.

I am pleased to acknowledge the gift, or loan for copying, of many pictures over the years. Those whose originals are used in this book are: Mrs Alice Barratt, Mr Fred Barratt, Mrs Beryl Bennett, the late Mr Tom Blaxland, Mrs Margaret Brown, Mr Arthur Burgess, the late Mr E.J. Carter, Mr Robin Chapple, Mr Neville Collins, Mr John Currant, Mr David Dent, Mr Jack Edwards, Mr Bryn Elliott, Mr David Fairhurst, the Revd Canon John Hasted, Mr Bob Hayden, the late Mr D.S. Hindell, the late Mr Tom Howlett, the late Mrs Joyce Kimsey, Mr Peter Manning, Mrs Jean Mullenger, the late Mr Hilary Norwood and Mrs Letty Norwood, the late Mr and Mrs Owen Oyler, Mr and Mrs Michael Petter, Mr Bryan Rochford, Mr Keith Rudling, Mrs May Shepherd, Mrs Marjorie Short, the late Mrs Snudden.

I apologise to anyone whose name is inadvertently omitted.

I am indebted to David Perman of Rockingham Press for commissioning this book and for his help and encouragement throughout its preparation.

Finally, a very personal "thankyou" to my wife Daphne, who has not only supported me in the preparation of this book but has encouraged me in my local history studies for over forty years.

The Eleanor Cross, on a postcard used in 1906. The Falcon was completely rebuilt in the 1890s after further work on the cross, so that traffic could encircle the monument. A sign proclaims the Falcon as "Headquarters, South Herts Automobile Club." There is just one car in the picture, and a bicycle, among various horse-drawn vehicles.

INTRODUCTION

This book covers the ancient parish and former Urban District of Cheshunt, which includes Waltham Cross, Goffs Oak and Turnford. Until well into the 20th century this scattered district consisted of little more than a ribbon of development along the Old North Road from the Middlesex boundary to the south to Wormley in the north, with isolated settlements around the parish church at Churchgate, at Flamstead End, and at Hammond Street and Goffs Oak on higher ground to the west. From the 1880s to the 1950s much of the land between these developed areas was covered with glasshouses.

Between the wars, and increasingly so after 1945, development was rapid. Most of the land once covered by nurseries is now under bricks and mortar. Large houses have been demolished for the development value of their grounds, sometimes after years of neglect, vandalism and arson. What were once separate settlements have merged into one. Several former Metropolitan Boroughs and the Greater London Council have built large estates for "overspill" population. Between 1951 and 1961 Cheshunt grew at a greater rate than any other place in England except for the designated New Towns. Improvement in transport links has hastened the spread of suburbs as more and more people commute to the capital.

Despite wholesale redevelopment of such areas as Cheshunt High Street, Holdbrook and central Waltham Cross, when much of historic interest was destroyed, some interesting buildings remain — especially in Churchgate, now a designated conservation area. The most frequently repeated words in this book are "demolition" and "redevelopment." This really sums up the last fifty years. The pictures show something of what has been lost to the built environment; they also speak of a quieter and less frenetic way of life.

CHESHUNT *in* 1807

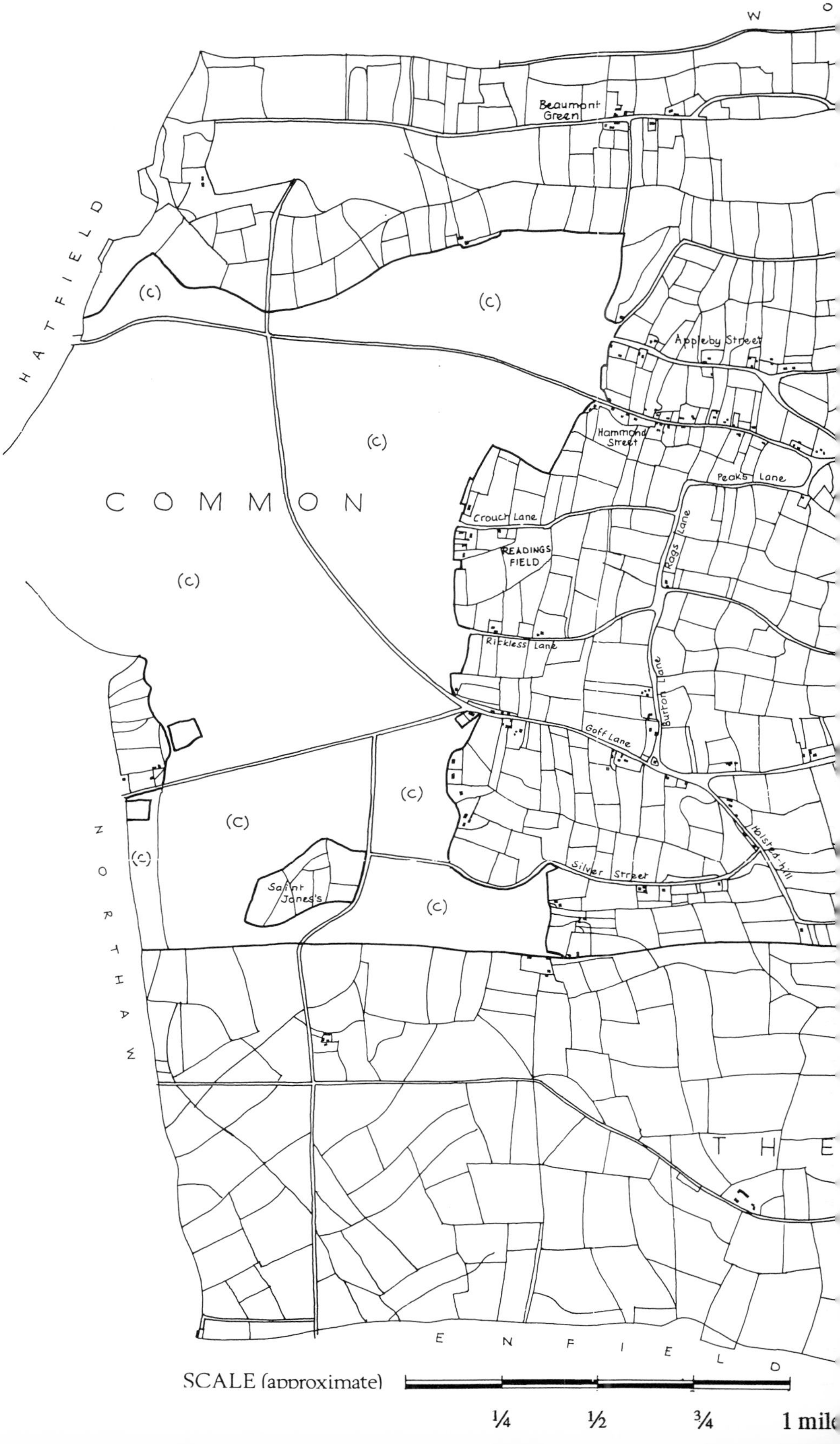

W O O

Beaumont
Green

HATFIELD

(c)

(c)

Appleby Street

Hammond
Street

Peaks Lane

(c)

Crouch Lane

C O M M O N

READINGS
FIELD

Rags Lane

(c)

Rickless Lane

Burton Lane

(c)

Goff Lane

(c)

Holsters hill

N O R T H A W

(c)

(c)

Silver Street

(c)

Saint Janes's

(c)

T H E

E N F I E L D

SCALE (approximate)

¼   ½   ¾   1 mile

BASED ON AN ORIGINAL MAP BY
HENRY CRAWTER IN CHESHUNT
PUBLIC LIBRARY

P.E. Rooke 1974

The Eleanor Cross photographed in 1860. The front of the Falcon was set back at an angle during the restoration of the cross in the 1830s, but there was no room for traffic to pass all round the cross. Compare this picture with that on page 7, showing the rebuilding in the 1890s to allow traffic to encircle the monument, and the picture opposite.

The Eleanor Cross and Four Swans in 1956. The further part of the pub has been demolished to make way for shops. Trolleybus wires surround the Eleanor Cross, which was restored again in 1950-53.

WALTHAM CROSS

The Eleanor Cross was built by King Edward I to commemorate the overnight stop of the cortege of his queen at Waltham Abbey in December 1290. He built the cross here so that it should be seen by travellers on the main road from London to the North. The High Street was lined with tenements by the 15th century: expansion westwards was blocked by the Theobalds lands, but the arrival of the railway in 1840 and the trams in 1908 prompted much development to the east. Waltham New Town (now called Holdbrook) was built up in the mid-19th century with cottages for workers at the Royal Gunpowder Factory just across the Essex border.

Aerial view of Waltham Cross, 1926. High Street runs across the picture, Eleanor Cross Road goes off to the right. Clearly visible are the Four Swans and the Falcon left and right of the Eleanor Cross, the Imperial Hall in Eleanor Cross Road, and the tramlines ending at the gates of Gwendoline House. Many properties have long rear gardens or ranges of stabling.

The Four Swans was demolished in the late 1960s as part of the redevelopment which gave us the shopping pavilion and multi-storey car park. The Eleanor Cross stood in temporary isolation. The Falcon was demolished in about 1978, although its site was not redeveloped for about ten years.

Above: Almshouses, High Street, at the parish boundary on the east side of the street. They were built in 1830 on the site of an ancient "spital." An extra tenement was added in 1903 (the new brickwork on the left of this 1905 picture), but all were rebuilt further back in 1908 to allow for road widening. The site is now occupied by the M25 motorway.

Below: York Road, about 1906; the main street of the Queen Eleanor estate, built between 1877 and the 1890s. Convenient for the station, it was largely occupied by managerial and clerical commuters. This street became a rat-run for vehicles, now discouraged by traffic management.

Waltham Cross Station G. E. R.

Above: Waltham Cross station in Edwardian days. The proximity of this station encouraged Anthony Trollope to live at Waltham House: from here he travelled to his Post Office work and his clubs and literary friends in London. It appears that commuters were met at the station with transport even ninety years ago.

Below: Station Road, about 1905, looking towards Waltham Abbey along what is now a dual carriageway highway through Holdbrook. The houses on the left were for commuting businessmen, while many cottages in the culs-de-sac on the right were lived in by Gunpowder Factory workers.

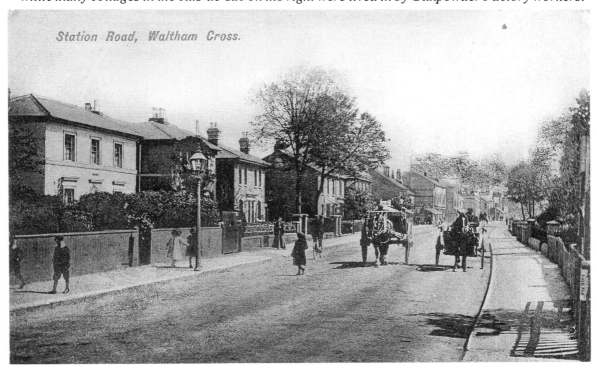

Station Road, Waltham Cross.

Above: High Street, Waltham Cross, 1948, looking south towards Fishpool's store. The road sweeper has his trolley across the street. The three-storey block was built just before the 1939-45 war but the shops were not fitted out until the time of this photo.

Below: High Street, Waltham Cross, about 1905, looking north towards Theobalds Grove railway bridge. The gas lamp on the right stands at the corner of Eleanor Road. Monarch's Way now swings off here and none of these buildings remain.

Above: Theobalds Grove railway bridge, looking south, in 1955. Theobalds Lane on the right, the turrets of Holy Trinity Church above the bridge on the left. E.J. Woollard advertises "smoke generators and spraying oils for use under glass."

Opposite, top: Middle Row, High Street, Waltham Cross, looking south. These narrow houses stood just south of Hedworth Avenue, and as in other towns may have been the successors of market stalls. Photo of about 1928.

Opposite, bottom: High Street, Waltham Cross, about 1890, looking north from just south of Park Lane. The road is not tarred and there are no kerbs. The Post Office was perhaps the most imposing building in the street. The butcher's shop has a canopy to shade its window. Two quite young boys by the wooden horse trough are wearing bowler hats.

THEOBALDS
BIRD'S EYE VIEW FROM THE EAST

Theobalds Palace: a bird's eye view from the east. There are no authentic contemporary pictures of the Palace; this reconstruction is based on Sir John Summerson's researches. It consisted of a series of three courtyards surrounded by buildings of increasing height and splendour.

Old Palace House. One of the houses built on the Palace site, this one contained at least two original Elizabethan windows. When it burnt down soon after purchase by Cheshunt Council in 1968, one of these windows was kept as a rather sad reminder of a charming house.

THEOBALDS

Cedars Park covers the site of the Royal Palace of Theobalds, built by William Cecil Lord Burghley in the 16th century and largely demolished during Cromwell's Commonwealth. It was one of the largest houses in England and was the prototype of several other mansions of the time. In the 18th century its site was occupied by a number of gentlemen's villas, all of which (except parts of The Cedars) have now gone. In the 1920s Admiral Meux gave most of the site to Cheshunt Council for use as a public park, and the Council purchased Old Palace House in 1968.

Theobalds Park, west of the A.10, was built by the Prescott family in the 1760s. From the 1820s it was tenanted, then owned, by the brewing family of Meux. Since the death of Admiral of the Fleet Sir Hedworth Meux in 1929 it has been used as a hotel, school and college, and may soon re-open as a hotel.

Above: Theobalds Lane, about 1890, looking east towards Crossbrook Street. On the right the entrance to a third house on the Palace site, usually known as Jackson's School — long since demolished, though the railings remain. Before the A.10 was built this lane gave direct access to Theobalds Park via Temple Bar, and was a private gated road.

Opposite, top: The Cedars, another of the 18th century villas, burned down in about 1912. A small wing and the conservatories remain. When this picture was taken in 1957 one of the magnificent Cedars of Lebanon still survived.

Opposite, bottom: Cedars Park, about 1925, looking towards the gate. This view shows Cecil House across Theobalds Lane on the corner of Albury Walk.

Above: Theobalds Park, east front, painted by J.C. Buckler about 1830. This shows the house as built by George Prescott in the 1760s; its elevated situation gave sylvan views across landscaped grounds, the New River (in the foreground) and over the Lea Valley to the Essex hills (Picture: Herts County Record Office).

Oposite, top: Theobalds Park, east front, 1937. To the original house have been added the tower and domestic quarters at the south end (by Sir H.B. Meux in 1887) and the ballroom wing at the north end (by Admiral Meux in about 1912).

Opposite, bottom: Theobalds Park, west front, about 1895. At the north end was a huge conservatory: in 1915 a party of naval midshipmen passed over in a balloon, pulled down a chimney with their grappling hook and demolished the glasshouse. Admiral Meux was not best pleased.

Above: Theobalds Park: the entrance hall in 1937, when the house was used as a hotel. One of the best Georgian interiors in the district, the ceiling is painted in the Etruscan style. Together with other ground floor rooms this has been magnificently restored recently.

Opposite, top: Theobalds Park: the panelled room, 1937. This was used by Lady Valerie Meux as the dining room, with a table 18 feet by 5 and twenty Charles I style chairs. The Jacobean style panelling was brought from a house at Dauntsey.

Opposite, bottom: Temple Bar, about 1895. Removed from The Strand in 1877, Sir H.B. Meux acquired the stones and had them re-erected at Theobalds Park (with a new gatekeeper's lodge) in 1887-8. Lady Valerie could now boast the finest front gate in England.

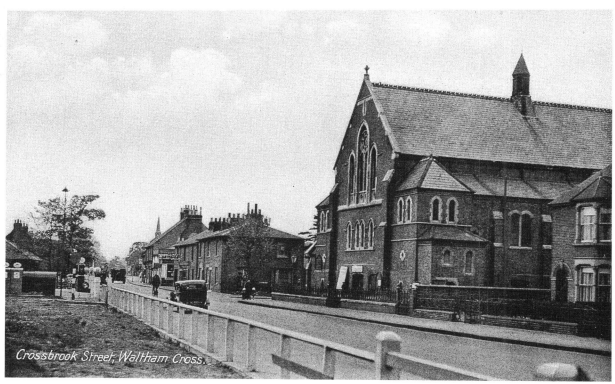

Crossbrook Street, Waltham Cross.

A view of Crossbrook Street, looking north, about 1905. The site of the Congregational Church is now occupied by the Bristol and West Building Society offices. In those days children could stand in the road for the photographer's benefit.

CROSSBROOK STREET

The northward continuation of the Old North Road was named after the minor manor of Cressbrookes, also known as Darcies, which was on the east side of the road.

Opposite, top: Theobalds Lane corner, about 1890. This was the main entrance to Theobalds Park and was only a permissive right of way. The pretty little gatekeeper's lodge probably dated from the mid-19th century; there were similar lodges at other entrances to the estate.

Opposite, bottom: Another northward view of Crossbrook Street, about 1935. The Methodist Church stands on the corner of Cecil Road, and opposite are the petrol pumps of Morris and Carr's garage.

Above: Houses on the east side of Crossbrook Street, north of the Bristol and West building. One was dated 1694: they were replaced in the 1960s by the office block Valley House. Photo of about 1910.

Below: Crossbrook Street looking south from the Roman Urn, about 1905. Remarkably, this frontage is basically unchanged today. The unique inn sign is thought to be, in fact, a Grecian vessel dug up nearby.

Above: Albury Ride, about 1910. This turning off Crossbrook Street was originally an entrance to the common field of Albury. The villas date from the 1890s and Edwardian days; the south side was not developed until the 1930s.

Below: Crossbrook Street — a row of (perhaps) 17th century cottages adjoining Brook Bakery. They were demolished about 1960 for the development of Laburnum Close.

This row of Georgian houses with shops added at the front was demolished in the early 1960s for building the Lynton Parade shops — demolition of Barratt's the greengrocers had already taken place. The house with the gable was once a college for working women.

TURNERS HILL

Continuing north we pass into Turners Hill, known in 1669 as Pembrooke or Pentbrooke Street. One wonders who Turner was, and the hill is hardly perceptible. It includes the shopping centre at the Old Pond, named after a pond (fed by the College Road brook) which was filled in by order of the Board of Health in the 1850s.

Opposite, top: Elm Arches in 1948, with the ground floor in use as the Food Office. This fine 18th century house with extensive grounds was given to Cheshunt Council by the Grundy brothers in 1911-13. It passed into the hands of developers and in August 1989 there was a fire on an upper floor. The entire building was then demolished with unseemly haste.

Opposite, bottom: Elm Arches from Grundy Park at the rear, about 1935. Not so attractive from this side, but still a great loss to the street scene.

Above: The Old Pond, 1928, the year the three-storey Barclays building was erected. An open-topped No. 69 bus is bound for Camberwell Green. By the gas lamp on the left is a fire alarm and a hydrant.

Below: The Old Pond pub, about 1905. At the College Road junction there was, until 1960, a triangle of land with buildings on it; here we see the Cricketers pub with a signboard above the eaves.

Above: The Old Pond, about 1905, looking north. On the left is the triangle with yet another pub, the Rifleman. The hydrant has its tall pipe for filling the watercarts which sprayed the dusty roads. The thatched cottage on the right is now occupied by Martins the newsagents and Junipers the opticians.

Below: The Old Pond: Clydesdale Villas, about 1910. The centre one was the offices of the Freehold Land & Building Corporation, with the Burial Board to the right. These are now the shops of Tandy and Safedale Pharmacy.

Above: Turners Hill, about 1910. Aug. J. Hall, printer and bookbinder; Brown, family grocer; J.F. Norris, barber; a draper's shop, and the George pub. Beyond the George sign a poster advertises Daisy Jerome at the Palace Cinema, Waltham Cross (later the Regent).

Opposite, top: The Old Pond, about 1920. These premises adjoined the Midland Bank, where Newnham Parade now is. Chas. Bunce later moved his printing works to Holt House in Flamstead End. The shop to the right is that of J.B. Gaze who later moved across the road to Clydesdale Villas in partnership with Mr Garside.

Opposite, bottom: Windmill Lane in 1956, looking towards the Midland Bank and Farmer Butcher (formerly Bellam's). The cottages were demolished for building the Wolsey Hall (opened 1961) and adjoining shops. On the right, the old stables at the rear of Crawter's premises.

Westlands, Turner's Hill, Cheshunt.

Above: Turners Hill, about 1905, looking south from the Old English Gentleman. Another late Victorian terrace, Westlands, on the left: the first unit is a saddlery and harness shop. Opposite is P. Burgess the blacksmith and H.C. Walsh's cycle and motor works. Walsh is said to have built the first motor taxi-cab.

Opposite, top: Turners Hill, about 1905, looking north from the junction of the present Clarendon Road. Until the mid-19th century the main road ran down Gews Corner, emerging at Church Lane. This new length of road was quickly lined with villas: West View (1901) and Moray Place (1897) are seen here. On the left are the premises of Nicholas the funeral furnisher, where ECP Motors are today.

Opposite, bottom: Blindmans Lane, behind the Old English Gentleman; 1919 photo of part of a fine group of 17th century cottages, demolished for road widening in 1939. The board on the left gable advertises J.F. Eaton, coal merchant. There is a drinking fountain, a granite horse trough, and another hydrant. The children have a box-on-pramwheels cart.

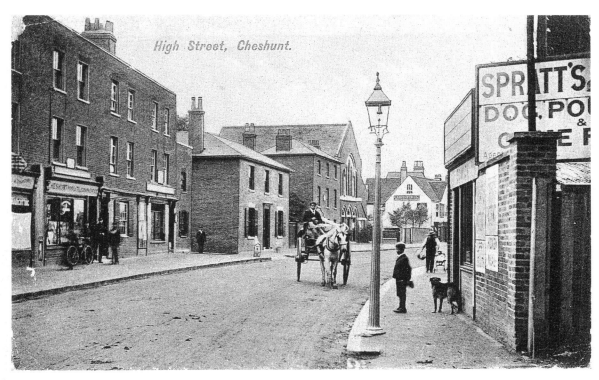

Above: High Street, looking north, about 1905. A group of messenger boys stand outside the Post Office. Further along are the United Reformed Church and the Haunch of Venison pub.

Below: Heaton House stood where the Heaton Court flats are today. Another good Georgian house sacrificed to redevelopment. This photo from the rear garden was taken about 1910.

*High Street looking north from near Church Lane, about 1910. The large grocery shop of C. &
A. Blaxland was where the Gateway supermarket now is. Mrs Elliott kept the shop at No. 5; her
daughter taught for many years at St Mary's School. The milk cart is Groombridge's from Penton
House Dairy Farm.*

HIGH STREET, CHESHUNT

Still called by its old name of Chesthunt Street by some locals, this length of the Old North Road
has been built up since medieval days — though little of any age now remains. The north end, from
Cadmore Lane to Brookfield Lane, was almost entirely destroyed and rebuilt by the Council in the
1960s — that great era of "redevelopment."

Above: No. 46 High Street, photographed in 1957. Formerly known as Wycliffe House and occupied by Tom Bones, the nurseryman and florist, this 18th century wooden building with nice detailing has been replaced by an undistinguished row of modern shops. Far right is Bishop and Cain's shop, still standing.

Below: High Street, northwards from the Haunch of Venison: a postcard used in 1904. Taylor the butcher has a canopy across the pavement opposite Wycliffe House.

Above: High Street looking south, about 1930. The two shops on the right have gas lamps above their windows; the newsagent offers "Tit-Bits every Saturday—2d."

Below: Where Warwick Drive now runs off the High Street. Ernest Paul, another nurseryman and florist, had this shop and fascinating house with a 17th century core. The Woolpack pub far left. This photo was taken in 1948.

Above: High Street at the north end in about 1960. The Anchor pub remains, the other properties await demolition — including, regrettably, Sharpe's fish shop, which bore a very fine moulded brick cartouche dated 1689.

Opposite, top: High Street, east side, north of Cadmore Lane — an area now completely cleared and rebuilt. This 1948 picture shows the Horse and Groom, Ramus' cycle shop and the 16th century premises of Lawrance the wheelwright. There is a delivery door at first floor level.

Opposite, bottom: West side of High Street, 1948, showing the Come Again Stores in what appears to have been a timber-framed building. Beyond it is the Ship, beside which Ship Alley ran to the Great Cambridge Road — and originally into Brook Field.

Turnford Hall, 1951; this Georgian house was bought in the 1880s by the Rochfords, who built nurseries in its grounds. Last occupied by Mr George Rochford, it was demolished in the 1960s and the site redeveloped.

TURNFORD

This "endship" of Cheshunt, originally a small hamlet, began to grow in the late 19th century with the arrival of Rochford's nurseries. Since the last war new housing estates have replaced all the nurseries and there is no visual break between Cheshunt and Turnford, or between Turnford and Wormley to the north.

Opposite, top: Cheshunt Wash in 1948. This part of the main road is flanked by streams which often flooded in the past. On the left, one corner of Thomas Rochford's glasshouses. The aerial conveyor brought gravel excavated east of the railway to the hoppers, from which lorries were loaded. St Clement's Church is on the right.

Opposite, bottom. High Road in 1956, showing nursery workers cycling home for lunch. On the left is Turnford Hall at the corner of Nunsbury Drive; beyond is the Old Bull's Head.

Above: The stables and coach-house of Nunsbury, photographed in 1957. Together with the house it was demolished in about 1960 to make way for East Herts (now Hertford Regional) College. The clock is now in Lowewood Museum.

Opposite, top: High Road near the Wormley boundary, looking south, 1955. On the left are Spring Cottages, housing Rochford's workers: on the right is West Side, built in 1929-32. In the foreground is part of Rochford's sports field, now built up as The Butts and The Oval.

Opposite, bottom: More Rochford cottages, south of Nursery Road. The corner shop was also the sub-Post Office for Turnford: to the right, the sign of the Bull's Head. From a postcard of about 1910.

High Road, Turnford

College Road, Cheshunt.   No. 3287.

College Road, Cheshunt.

College Road, from a card used in 1907, looking east and showing the street passing either side of the triangle. On the right is St Mary's Hall; comparison with the picture on page 50 shows that in its conversion to a cinema various "Jacobean" embellishments were removed.

COLLEGE ROAD

Running west from Turners Hill to Churchgate and Bury Green, this road was known as Water Lane until mid-Victorian times. It is the route to western Cheshunt, Goffs Oak and Cuffley.

Opposite, top: College Road looking west in the 1950s. The Central Cinema, demolished in the mid-1960s, was previously St Mary's Hall. With a small bellcote is the British School, built in 1857 and superseded just after the war by Burleigh School; it was converted to offices and small shops in 1979.

Opposite, bottom: College Road looking east from Blindmans Lane, 1957. On the right are The Old Grange (now an old people's home) and Cheshunt Cottage. Opposite is the 18th century White House, now replaced by a modern terrace. The cedar tree remains, minus some of its lower branches.

Marina Gardens Cheshunt

134994

Above: Blindmans Lane looking north from College Road just before road widening in 1939. On the right is the site of Burleigh School; on the extreme left are the chimnies of The Clock House.

Opposite, top: The Grange, College Road, from the rear in 1924. This once famous garden was described by J.C. Loudon in the Gardener's Magazine in 1839, but is now covered by the houses of Littlebrook Gardens.

Opposite, bottom: Marina Gardens, off Blindmans Lane, just after its completion in 1935: it was named after Princess Marina of Greece who married the Duke of Kent in 1934. The small hut on the left may be an estate agent's office.

Cheshunt. College Road

Above: The Red House, College Road, about 1937: an early 18th century house which stood on the site of the present College Court. Badly damaged by wartime bombing, it had to be demolished; its owner (seen here), the Revd B.J. Haddad, moved to Cheshunt Great House.

Opposite, top: Grange Cottages, College Road, in 1919. Formerly Water Lane Farmhouse, this mid-16th century house was occupied by staff from The Grange. Now two separate houses, it has changed very little externally.

Opposite, bottom: College Road looking west, about 1910. In the centre is Archer's builder's yard, and beyond it the row of cottages which included the old Crocodile pub. The A10 now cuts across the foreground.

Arterial Road, Cheshunt

Above: College Road crossroads, looking south, in 1929 - about five years after the building of the single-carriageway Great Cambridge Road (now the A10). No traffic lights, but an A.A. box and patrolman, and a filling station where J.R. Enterprises are now.

Below: The same view in the mid-1930s. There are now traffic lights, and ribbon development has begun along the new road. The second carriageway was not built until the late 1960s.

Cross Roads Cheshunt

Above: The Sweep's Cottage, College Road, where the entrance to Cheshunt School is now: photo of about 1925. The writer's grandfather used to borrow Teddy Dowman's donkey, cart and chimney brushes for the annual Bakers and Sweeps football match.

Right: The New River bridge, College Road, in about 1920. The bridge was rebuilt and the road greatly widened in 1939.

Church Lane, Cheshunt.

Hatton House, Church Lane, built in 1754. This photo of 1951 shows the original wrought iron gate and railings, removed some years later for road widening. Then a private residence, now in office use.

CHURCH LANE

Leading west from Cheshunt High Street, Church Lane runs to Flamstead End and, at one time via Andrews Lane and St James' Road, to Goffs Oak. Until 1950 there was still agricultural land at Kilsmore Farm.

Opposite, above: Church Lane looking east in about 1930. In the middle distance is the castellated late Georgian Castle Villa, where Hobbs Close runs now. The Cottage Hospital entrance is at the left.

Opposite, bottom: Cheshunt Cottage Hospital was built by public subscription and opened by Lady Meux in 1889; it was extended in 1910, with new buildings added more recently. Now closed and awaiting demolition.

Above: Church Lane looking west, about 1930. Dewhurst Road now goes off to the left where the cyclist is. The kissing gate at the right led to a footpath across Dandy White's Fields (Kilsmore Farm).

Below: Looking down Church Lane from its western end, about 1927, with the Jolly Bricklayers on the corner of Flamstead End Road. Mr Fuller kept the sweet shop, where the writer spent his boyhood pocket money.

The Old Parsonage, with cottages opposite, in 1902. Of similar plan, these date from the late 15th or early 16th century. The one on the right is believed to have been damaged by Zeppelin bombs: it was ruinous in the summer of 1918 and was demolished the following year.

CHURCHGATE

The area round the Parish Church is the ancient village of Cheshunt. On the site of St Mary's High School was the manor house, later known as The Lordship. Although some good buildings have gone since the war, this is now a designated Conservation Area.

Church Gate Corner, Cheshunt. No. 2273.

Grove Cottage from the garden, drawn by Raymond Newell for "Radio Times" in about 1948 when the BBC were serialising "The Small House at Allington" on the radio. (Picture: Radio Times).

Opposite, top: The corner of Churchgate and Cromwell Avenue in about 1925, looking towards Grove Cottage. This is believed to be the house on which Trollope modelled "The Small House at Allington." It was owned by Bishops' College, who sold it for redevelopment in the early 1960s; Bishops' Court now occupies the site.

Opposite, bottom: Pengelly Lodge, Churchgate (opposite Grove Cottage) in 1953. This was the last building associated with Pengelly House, which burned down in 1888. The lodge fell to the bulldozer in 1977.

The Dining Hall, Bishops' College, Cheshunt.

Above: Bishops' College dining room in about 1914. This is now known as the Huntingdon Suite and is available for hire for private functions. This part of the building dates from 1820.

Below: The New River skirts the grounds of Bishops' College. Constructed between 1608 and 1613 to bring fresh water to London from springs near Ware, it is a picturesque feature in many areas. The small gazebo in this 1950s picture was demolished by Broxbourne Council in 1983.

CHT.31 New River, CHESHUNT

The Architect, Dec.ʳ. 31.ˢᵗ 1870.

CHESHUNT COLLEGE,
NEW BUILDINGS.
MESSʳˢ LANDER & BEDELLS, ARCHITECTS.

Scale for Plan.
0   10 20 30 40 50 60 70 80 90 100 110 120 FEET

Bishops' College. The nonconformist Cheshunt College was here from 1792 to 1905, when it moved to Cambridge. In 1875 the octagon (which housed the library), tower and east wing were built to the above design by Lander and Bedells, except for the cloister at the left. A Church of England theological college, Bishops' College, occupied the premises from 1909 to 1968: they were bought by Cheshunt Council in 1972 and a large extension for the offices of Broxbourne Council was opened by the Duke of Kent in 1986.

Above: Whit Hern, Churchgate. This house, an amalgam of styles from the 17th to 19th centuries, was bought by Cheshunt Council in 1956 so that its grounds could be used as a public park. Unfortunately the Council demolished the house, thereby losing an attractive building and punching a huge hole in the street picture. The fine early railings remain.

Below: Whit Hern garden viewed from an upstairs window, about 1938. The layout of the present park is very similar.

The Cottage, 106 Churchgate, seen from the garden in 1948. Partly 17th century with many later additions, this charming house retains its stable and carriage house, with dovecote and hayloft above.

Above:Homeleigh and adjoining cottages, Churchgate, 1957. Homeleigh, stuccoed and with a bow window, and the Georgian cottages with good doorcases, were demolished for road widening in 1969.

Below: Rear view of Homeleigh awaiting demolition in 1969.

"The Plough" Flamstead End Cheshunt.

The Plough, Flamstead End Road; this possibly 16th century building, with a real plough for its sign, was rebuilt in about 1920. The writer's grandfather trained a tug-of-war team for the coronation celebrations in 1911 using this tree as an anchor.

FLAMSTEAD END

Around the junction of Brookfield Lane, Longfield Lane and Flamstead End Road is the old settlement of Flamstead End — at one time truly an "end," but now absorbed into the town by new housing. In the first half of the 20th century it was at the centre of the local nursery industry.

Above: Molwallups, Park Lane, in 1957. For many years a Debenham property and occupied by Cheshunt Park retainers, it was demolished in the 1970s. The strange name is thought to mean "molehills."

Opposite, top: Flamstead End Road from the top of Church Lane, about 1905. The pond, filled in before 1931, was on the site of the present car park at the Jolly Bricklayers. The cottages on the left were demolished when the Fairley Way estate was built in 1919.

Opposite, bottom: The Pound, Flamstead End, about 1915. This enclosure on roadside manorial waste was for impounding stray cattle. A few posts remained until the late 1920s. The oak tree still stands at the gates of no. 6 Flamstead End Road.

Above: Thatched cottages north of the Plough, about 1905. They were demolished about 1965 for new houses. In the distance is the Greyhound Stores, built at the turn of the century.

Belowe: Flamstead End, looking south from the top of Brookfield Lane in about 1905. The cottages on both sides have been cleared for road widening and redevelopment. The vehicle on the right appears to be a water cart filling up at a hydrant.

The village pond at the corner of Newgatestreet Road, 1907. At the left is a corner of the smithy: left of centre is the Goffs Oak Hotel and the old oak.

GOFFS OAK

Still a separate (but very suburban) village, Goffs Oak originated as a cluster of cottages on the edge of Cheshunt Common. Usually said to take its name from the ancient tree, it is referred to in some old documents as Goffs Hatch, i.e. Goffs Gate - perhaps because of its position at the entrance to the common.

Goffs Lane, Goffs Oak.

108224.

Above: Goffs Oak police houses, still in the hands of the builders, 1895 — with, apparently, a tenant waiting to move in! These houses still stand by the war memorial, but are now privately owned.

Opposite, top: Goffs Lane looking west towards the village in about 1925. The Wheelwrights is on the left; this was succeeded by a modern pub across the road in the 1970s. Many cottages in this area were destroyed by a German "doodlebug" in 1944, and the road was later widened.

Opposite, bottom: The old oak tree, photo of 1889. To the right is the Goffs Oak Hotel. The tree is said to have been planted to commemorate the Norman Conquest in 1066; it was obviously very ancient, and 100 years ago was still quite vigourous. It later became smothered with ivy and blew down in 1950. Charles Lamb mentioned it in a letter.

Above: Goffs Oak looking west, about 1910. At the road fork is the smithy, and in front of it a small hose-reel shed for the fire brigade. The Post Office later moved to Newgatestreet Road, but is now back in the same shop.

Below: Newgatestreet Road, looking north, about 1920. According to the caption this was then known as Mill Road. This picture was taken before the building of Goffs Oak Avenue.

The Avenue, Goff's Oak.

Above: Goffs Oak Avenue, a cul-de-sac of houses built by Cheshunt Council in 1923. This picture appears to date from soon after work was completed.

Below: Goffs Oak Windmill and the mill house, 1902. The mill was built about 1860 and was working until the 1890s. The sails and cap blew off between 1918 and 1921, and the last traces of the tower disappeared in the 1950s. It stood at the eastern end of The Crest.

Goff's Oak Church & Schools

Above: St James' Road, Goffs Oak, about 1910. Known as Rickless Lane before the building of St James' Church in 1862. The school has now been converted to a private house.

Below: Rags Lane, Goffs Oak, about 1910. To the left is the boundary fence of Burton Grange. The hedge on the right conceals "Boundary Bank," an ancient ditch and bank which might have been the boundary of a parish — or even a kingdom. The three workmen are Joe Danton, Jack Hobson and Walter Eames.

A Lane near Newgate Street

Cheshunt Great House: fireplace in the hall, on a postcard used in 1915. The notices on the armour say "Visitors are requested not to touch."

THE BIG HOUSE

From the time of Lord Burghley's purchase of Theobalds Cheshunt became popular as a country retreat for minor gentry and City businessmen. Few of their houses now remain; many have fallen to the developers, while others have proved uneconomic to keep up. Just three of them are mentioned here.

Above: Cheshunt Great House, Goffs Lane. Originally the manor house of Andrews and le Motte, its core dated from the late 15th century. Once owned by Cardinal Wolsey, it was reduced in size and encased in Georgian brick by the Shaw family in 1750. Through most of the 19th century and until the 1930s it was a freemasons' hall.

Below: Cheshunt Great House: the 15th century hall as it was in 1884. The door at the far left corner led to two-storey living quarters at the rear.

Above: After several changes of ownership The Great House went up in flames in suspicious circumstances one night in September 1965. The site was bought by the GLC and included in their Rosedale development: the old people's flats of Peace Close now encircle the conserved undercroft — all that is left of the most historic house in the district.

Below: The Revd B.J. Haddad occupied the Great House from just after the last war until his death in 1957. A priest of the Church of England as well as a dealer in pianos and antiques, he created his own chapel in the medieval undercroft of the house.

Above: Cheshunt Park was built in 1795 by Oliver Cromwell, London solicitor and descendant of the Lord Protector. His descendant leased it in 1865, with its 600 acres of land, to F.G. Debenham, a London estate agent. In 1918 his four unmarried daughters purchased the freehold: they later sold off much of the agricultural land north of the house, and after the death of the last surviving sister in 1968 the residue was bought by Cheshunt Council for public open space and a golf course. The house, photographed here in about 1950, was promptly demolished.

Left: The First Lodge, Cheshunt Park. Cromwell built at least three lodges on the fringes of the estate. This one was in Park Lane just past the present entrance to the golf course. It fell into disrepair and was demolished in the late 1960s.

The Second Lodge at Cheshunt Park, at the entrance of what was the back drive to the big house, in about 1960. Its walls are faced with pebbles, glass, tree bark and other materials. This little gem, luckily, survives.

Above: The Gamekeeper's Lodge, Park Lane Paradise. The uprights of the walls were tree trunks. Charlie Rumney the gamekeeper stands in his garden, about 1935. This building has gone.

Opposite, top: Waltham House, which stood on the east side of High Street, Waltham Cross, between Eleanor Cross Road and Abbey Road. Anthony Trollope lived here from 1859 to 1871, using one wing for his office as Eastern District Surveyor to the Post Office. The grounds extended to the railway. Rear view photo, 1900. (Country Life)

Opposite, bottom: The library of Waltham House: the shelving was Trollope's, but the books in this 1900 photo were the horticultural library of the renowned rose grower William Paul. Later a convent school, the house was demolished in the 1930s when Abbey Road was built through its grounds. (Country Life)

Walton.   Printed by C. Hullmand

CHESHUNT CHURCH.

The Parish Church of St Mary the Virgin, Churchgate, was built in the early 15th century on the site of an earlier church. The churchyard was used for burials until the opening of the cemetery in Bury Green in 1855. This picture, of about 1860, is the earliest known photo of it. It shows the priest's door into the chancel before the south chapel was added in 1872-3.

CHURCHES

The ancient parish of Cheshunt, served by the Church of St Mary the Virgin at Churchgate, originally included Waltham Cross, Goffs Oak and Turnford. Nonconformity was strong in the district from the time that King James I owned Theobalds, and was strengthened by the presence of the Countess of Huntingdon's Cheshunt College throughout the 19th century.

Opposite, top: St Mary's Church from the north, from a lithograph of about 1840. This, the only copy ever seen by the writer, was sent by a former Cheshunt resident now living in South Africa.

Opposite, bottom: Interior of St Mary's, about 1890 - with the 1887 chancel screen but without the present organ of 1891. The stencilled wall decorations, done in 1883-4, are still fresh and clear. The stone traceried reredos reveals the full length of the east window.

Above: Holy Trinity Church, High Street, Waltham Cross, in about 1890. This was built as a chapel of ease to Cheshunt Church in 1832 and became the parish church of the new parish of Waltham Cross in 1855. It was extended in 1915. Since 1975 the building has been shared with the Methodists and known as Christ Church.

Above: St Clement's Church and School, Cheshunt Wash, Turnford, in 1956. The school (right) was opened in 1893 and the church in 1898. The site was the gift of John Earley Cook. The church was extended in 1980.

Below: Methodist Church, Crossbrook Street. There was a Methodist congregation in Cheshunt as early as 1808, but this church was not built until 1901. Since 1975 the Methodists and Anglicans have shared the use of Christ Church, and this building is now used by the Jehovah's Witnesses.

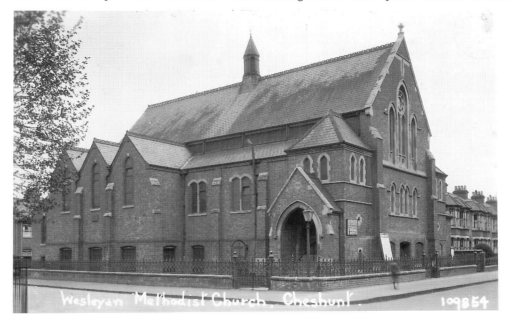

St James' Church, Goffs Oak, was built in 1862 to serve the western part of Cheshunt parish. It cost £3,750 to build, on a site acquired for £50. Goffs Oak became a separate parish in 1871.

Above: Congregational Church, Crossbrook Street, was built in 1857 on the site of an earlier chapel associated with Isaac Watts. In the 1960s it became a Roman Catholic centre known as Pope John Hall: in 1976 it was demolished for an extension of the Cheshunt Building Society offices. This picture of about 1930 also shows The Limes, a late Georgian house now converted to flats.

Left: United Reformed Church, High Street, Cheshunt. An independent chapel was established here in 1782. It was rebuilt in 1889, when it joined the Countess of Huntingdon's Connexion. In 1921 it united with a Baptist congregation and became known as Cheshunt Union Church; in 1972 it joined the new United Reformed Church. Extensive internal alterations are under way in 1994.

St Joseph's Church   Waltham X

Roman Catholic Church, on the corner of Eleanor Road. The first Catholic priest was appointed to Waltham Cross in 1859: from 1860 to 1865 worship was held in a High Street house. A church (now the church hall) was built in Eleanor Road in 1865, to be superseded by the present Church of the Immaculate Conception and St Joseph in 1931.

Holt House School, Flamstead End, the building later occupied by a printing works and replaced by flats in the 1980s. The school closed in the 1920s. This photo of about 1905 includes many boys who later became well known locally — Owen Oyler, P.W. Hargreaves, T.R. Trounce, and Tom Blaxland.

EDUCATION

Until the beginning of the 20th century education was provided by charities, the churches and private institutions. The County Council became education authority under the Education Act of 1902. Since the post-war population explosion so many new schools have been built that it is possible to deal here only with some of the older ones.

Above: Holy Trinity School, Trinity Lane. Two separate schools, one for boys and one for girls and infants, opened in 1841 on land given by the Vicar of Cheshunt, M.M. Preston. The School moved in 1952 to a new site in Crossbrook Street, and this photo shows the old buildings awaiting demolition. The site, behind Christ Church, now contains an office block.

Opposite, top: St Mary's School, Churchgate. A church school for infants and girls was built in 1872 and enlarged in 1913. This picture of about 1920 shows studious infants with Miss Green (left) and Miss Kent.

Opposite, bottom: St Clement's School, Turnford: a class with Miss Janet Blake in 1962. The school was opened by the Church authorities in 1893 to cater for the new influx of nursery workers and to relieve pressure on the Churchgate schools. It was extended in 1970-71 as a result of yet more housing development.

King's Road
SCHOOL
Orchestra.
WALTHAM CROSS

Above: Cheshunt Modern School, Windmill Lane. Built in 1938 and later much extended, this school changed its name to Cheshunt County School. Cheshunt Grammar School, and finally (on becoming a comprehensive) Cheshunt School. It removed to the former Bishopslea campus in College Road in 1992 and the future of the original building is not yet known. Photo of 1938.

Opposite, top: Kings Road School, Waltham Cross, was built by the County Council in 1913 to serve the Queen Eleanor estate and surrounding areas. This 1928 photo shows the school orchestra - not a common feature in schools at that time. Seated centrally is the Headmaster, Mr H.C. Cooper, who became prominent in local political life. Superseded by nearby Four Swannes School, the old buildings were burnt out in 1976.

Opposite, bottom: Cheshunt Modern School: the first school group photo, summer term 1938. Staff: Mr Poole (groundsman), Mr Taylor (caretaker), H. Norwood, W.G. Hyett, L.F. Roberts, R.J. Moxom (Headmaster), Miss M.H. Hughes (Senior Mistress), Miss G. Chapman, Miss M. Amiot, Miss W.M. Almrott (secretary), Mrs Taylor (caretaker's wife).

Above: Dewhurst School, Churchgate, photographed in 1919. Built and endowed by Robert Dewhurst, a wealthy lawyer, in 1640 for the benefit of local boys. Although controlled by the County Council since 1903, the Dewhurst Trustees still play an important role. In 1958 it merged with St Mary's School next door and is now known as Dewhurst St Mary School. The former Master's House has now been converted to flats.

Below: Dewhurst School: Class V in 1928, with Mr W. Coleman Edwards, Headmaster from 1924 to 1938.

The Hull mail coach at the Falcon, Waltham Cross; an 1832 print by James Pollard. From the 1780s to the advent of the railways the mail coaches, with their armed guards and privileged passage of turnpike gates, were the safest and quickest form of transport. Waltham Cross was the first "stage" from London and many coaches changed horses here.

TRANSPORT

Due north of London, on the Old North Road to York and Edinburgh, Cheshunt has always been subjected to much through traffic. The construction of the present A.10 in the 1920s brought some relief to the old high road. The Lea Valley became the natural route for the Lee Navigation canal and the main Cambridge railway line. The proximity of junction 25 on the M.25 motorway now funnels even more traffic along local roads.

Above: The Lee Navigation Canal. A navigable river from early times, the Lea was partially canalised in the 18th century. There was a wharf at the bottom of Windmill Lane but the canal was not so important to the local economy as it was to Ware and Hertford. This photo shows Cheshunt Lock in about 1910.

Below: Sailing barges on the Lea at Cheshunt, about 1890. Obviously the masts were collapsible to enable passage under bridges. As early as the 16th century barges were pulled along by men, but the usual form of traction was by horse. Many riverside pubs had stabling for barge horses.

Cheshunt Station in about 1900, looking down the line. The down platform was then north of the level crossing. The footbridge survives today. The completion of the line to Broxbourne in 1840 and Bishops Stortford in 1842 had far-reaching effects on the development of the district.

Above: An electric tram at the terminus in Waltham Cross High Street, just south of the Eleanor Cross. This postcard was used in 1911. The tramway reached Waltham Cross in January 1908, when it became possible for workmen to travel any distance for one penny, provided the journey was completed before 8 a.m.

Opposite, top: The first motor bus service from Waltham Cross to Angel Road began in August 1906 —before the tram service—but was short lived. This picture of about 1925 shows an open-topped "Primrose" bus, operated by G.A. Adams of Islington, waiting in York Road. Many of these smaller operators were absorbed by London Transport in 1933.

Opposite, bottom: Trolleybuses at their terminus in Eleanor Cross Road. The trams were replaced by trolleybuses in 1938, and the same vehicles continued in use until the routes were taken over by diesel buses in 1961. (Picture: David Fairhurst).

Above: The Waltham Gospel Temperance Brass Band, about 1910. In the days before radio and television, music making was a popular pastime. There were several bands in the district, including one for Rochford's employees at Turnford.

Below: Cheshunt Swimming Club, about 1930. This was at the pool beyond the railway in Windmill Lane, formed from a cut from the River Lea where Cheshunt Wharf had been. At the far right is Roland Archer the builder, for many years the club secretary.

Cheshunt Football Club, 1908-9 season. The photo is titled "Young and Old Sports." The writer's grandfather (third from right, centre row) was born in 1865, so could be classed as an "old sport."

LEISURE

Before many of became addicted to TV, entertainment was very largely home-made. Clubs proliferated, the Carnival was a great annual occasion. Many homes had a piano for family singsongs and amateur theatricals were very popular and well supported. Even a visit to the cinema required some effort. Children played happily at home and safely in the streets and fields.

Opposite: The Bakers and Sweeps football match, 1913. This Boxing Day tradition, begun a few years before, raised funds for Cheshunt Cottage Hospital. There are some well-known names here, including John Lawrence who was treasurer of the hospital.

Above: The 1955 Bakers and Sweeps match. Spot the ball! So much soot and flour is thrown that goal scoring is a minor consideration. This annual match is still played, to the benefit of local charities.

Above: Cheshunt Rugby Club in their first season, 1953-4, on Goffs Lane playing fields. The club consisted mostly of old boys of Cheshunt Grammar School and was called Old Cestrians in the early years. The club is now based at the Rosedale ground in Andrews Lane. Far right, David Bird; second right, Michael King; fourth right, John Payne.

Opposite, top: Comic cricket match (funny hats and wide bats) at Cheshunt Park, about 1930. The Misses Debenham maintained a fine pitch west of the house. Included here are the Edwards brothers (plumbers), John Cull, Tom Blaxland, Mr Fullom and F.H. Rudling the schoolmaster.

Opposite, bottom: The Church Lads Brigade at the Church Rooms, Churchfield Path, about 1914. At this period a quasi-military organisation — some of the boys have guns — the C.L.B. was strongly supported by the Vicar of Cheshunt, Charles Law (seated centre).

Above: A family at leisure—but carefully posed for the camera—about 1900. This is Mrs Bright, wife of the Waltham Cross blacksmith, with her children Charlie and Millie. There are pigeons in the aviary and various toys, including a dolls' tea-set.

Opposite, top: A pub outing—or a carnival entry?—outside the Four Swans. The postcard was used in August 1911, and as Union Jacks are in evidence this might have been connected with King George V's coronation in June 1911.

Opposite, bottom: Miss Mary Debenham's "Cheshunt Church Pageant" was performed in the grounds of Bishops' College in 1923. A slightly revised version was staged in 1936, when this picture was taken of actors waiting to go on. Fifth from the right is the Vicar of Cheshunt, R. Creed Meredith. (Picture: Hertfordshire Mercury).

Above: The Central Cinema, College Road, in 1955. Converted to a cinema before the first world war, this had been built as a public hall in 1862. For many years its "sole prop." was E.J. Carpenter. It closed in 1959 and was demolished in the mid-1960s for redevelopment with shops.

Below: The Embassy Cinema, Waltham Cross. This wonderful piece of art deco work was opened in 1937. It had a Christie organ, played before the war by Harold Betts, who became a well-known broadcaster. The Embassy was converted to four smaller auditoria in 1981 and closed in the early 1990s. It now stands empty. (Hertfordshire Publications/Premier Bioscope).

Building Theobalds Grove railway bridge, 1890. The Churchbury loop railway line was built to cater for an expected increase in traffic - which did not materialise. It closed to passenger traffic in 1905. But with post-war expansion and electrification of the railways it re-opened in 1960.

WORK

There was very little manufacturing industry in the district in the 19th century, although many local men and boys worked in the Gunpowder Factory at Waltham Abbey and the Royal Small Arms Factory at Enfield Lock — "The Lock." The nursery industry began to grow in the 1880s and by 1950 the district contained the largest area of glasshouses in the world. Since 1945 there has been diversification of employment, and with improved transport many people now go out of the district to work.

Above: A.C. Bright, with two employees, at his farrier's shop in Park Lane, Waltham Cross, about 1900. Little Millie gets into the picture again. One of Bright's workmen died of tetanus in 1902 after sustaining a minor injury at work.

Below: Bright's trade card of the 1890s, indicating that the business was of 18th century origin.

ESTABLISHED upwards of 100 YEARS.

A. C. BRIGHT,
(Late CHARLES COOMES.)
Farrier & Smith in General,
WALTHAM CROSS, HERTS.

Agent for the Yorkshire Veterinary Patent Medicine.

BICYCLES & TRICYCLES REPAIRED.

Above: Morris and Sons coach-building works, at the corner of High Street and Swanfield Road, Waltham Cross. In the late 1950s Bill and Bob Morris demonstrate the craft of tyring a cart wheel: Bill holds the tyre with tongs, while Bob is "dogging it on." The site was cleared soon after this picture was taken.

Below: The Morris and Sons bill-head, 1932. The Morrises did much work on the Enfield Highway Co-op's vehicles, grinding and mixing materials for the maroon paint to their own recipe.

ESTABLISHED 1808

M *Co-operative Society, Ltd.*   *Nov 29.th 1932.*

Dr. to G. MORRIS & SONS,

(LATE J. H. MOLD),

Coach Builders,
Waltham Cross.

Estimates given for all kinds
of Repairs.

Wheelmaking and Rubber Tyring
a speciality.

Bradbury, Motor Coach Printer, Harlesden, N.W.

1932.

Oct 25.th Green Grocer Trolley. 177.

Above: Waltham Cross Post Office staff, about 1900. Because of its position about 12 miles from the G.P.O. in London, Waltham Cross had been a post town since the reign of Henry VIII, and "Waltham Cross, Herts" is still the correct address for all the district except Turnford and Beaumont.

Below: Gravel digging on Seventy Acres Marsh, 1965. The development of large dragline excavators made it possible to bring gravel up from below the water, and since the war most of the Lea marshes have been worked over. The dragline here is depositing ballast in a barge for transport to the washing and screening plant at Fishers Green.

Strawberry picking, Theobalds Park Farm, 1913. George Oyler (in cap) and young Owen Oyler (in white hat). Owen carries a satchel of tokens, given to the pickers for each full basket and exchanged for wages at the end of the day.

Following pages: Nurseries between Goffs Lane and Longfield Lane, 1960. Andrews Lane runs diagonally from bottom right to top left. Right of centre is the 100-foot boiler chimney of Sandberg's nursery: most nurseries had small boilers heating about six glasshouses. Nearly all of this nursery land was acquired by the Greater London Council and developed for housing in the 1970s. (Picture: The Times).

Above: Melons in a Rochford's glasshouse in 1913. Before the great popularity of tomatoes, cucumbers and cut roses and carnations, some more exotic crops were grown. Rochford's were also famous for their grapes, long before becoming world leaders in house plants.

Opposite, top: For many years there was seasonal work for women. Here are two girls in one of Joseph Rochford's cucumber houses at Turnford in the first world war. At their waists are hanks of raffia for tying up the plants.

Opposite, bottom: Glasshouses after a hailstorm at Cheshunt in 1932. Nurserymen could insure against damage by hailstones; judging from this picture the premiums must have been pretty high.

Above: Elm Nursery, Longfield Lane, about 1920. This small nursery, specialising in bedding and pot plants, was started by the writer's grandfather (centre) in 1902. On the left are his sons Ted and George; one of the Pallett family (right) drove the horse-drawn van to Covent Garden Market. The nursery ceased trading in 1982 and is now covered by houses.

Below: Oakleigh Nursery (E. Stevens) between Longfield Lane and Andrews Lane, 1965. This nursery produced cut roses, and the thatched semi-sunken building served as a cool store and packing shed for the blooms. This was one of the nurseries soon to be sold to the G.L.C.

Above: Glasshouse soil needed frequent steam sterilisation. Steam passed along flexible pipes to metal grids and down hollow spikes pushed into the soil. After 20 minutes the grids were moved along. E. Stevens' nursery, Andrews Lane, 1953.

Below: From the 1950s to 1970s many hundreds of nursery jobs were lost as nurseries were cleared for housing estates. This 1957 picture, from Theobalds Grove station looking towards Cedars Park, shown glasshouses being demolished for the building of Dudley Avenue.

Above: The Fire Brigade, about 1930. From its formation in 1896 until its amalgamation into the National Fire Service in 1941 the fire brigade was run by Cheshunt Council. Here is what was probably its first motor fire engine, with its crew in brass helmets. Nearest the camera is Captain Sykes, who was also the Council's Sanitary Inspector from 1903 to 1938.

The Coronation of King Edward VII, 1902. A detachment of the Essex Yeomanry passes along Station Road, Waltham New Town, on its return from ceremonial duties in London. In the distance is the spire of St Cyprian's Church in Crescent Road (now Holdbrook North).

EVENTS

Any kind of spectacle seemed to draw large crowds of outsiders — weddings, funerals, football matches, flower shows. Some quite minor events were recorded on picture postcards. There were large-scale jollifications for jubilees, coronations, and other such national events as VE Day in 1945.

Above: The Bus Disaster, 2 August 1913. A party of workers from Hamilton's nursery at Waltham Cross had an outing to Cambridge, Robert Rice taking a group photo before they set out. On the way back the bus left the road and overturned just north of Hailey Lane, Hoddesdon, and five men were killed.

Below: Five horse-drawn hearses, accompanied by a huge crowd, brought the bodies for burial in a mass grave at Cheshunt Cemetery. The Vicar of Cheshunt, Charles Law, used the occasion to speak of the evils of strong drink - to the approval of the temperance lobby, but to the outrage of a great many others.

Above: The presentation of a British Mark V tank to Cheshunt Council was made in College Road, near the triangle, in 1921. It was displayed in Cedars Park until being sent for scrap to help win the second war in May 1940. The Council got £27 16s 10d for it.

Below: The official opening of Cheshunt Council's Franklin Avenue housing estate, 15 March 1933. The houses cost £291 each, including the land, roads and sewers. The speaker is Sir Francis Fremantle, M.P. for St Albans and former Medical Officer for Hertfordshire; he had also been chairman of the L.C.C. Housing Committee. Others on the platform include the Vicar (R.C. Meredith) and Councillor Bellam (the butcher).

Above: Goffs Oak Carnival, 1950. A sapling oak, grown by Mr Munns at the Post Office from an acorn of the original Goffs Oak, is being planted to replace the old tree which blew down earlier in the year. A few weeks later it disappeared — Council workmen had removed it in the mistaken belief that it was dead. A furious Mr Munns eventually agreed to supply another seedling, provided he supervised its planting and care. This one survived, and is now a good-sized tree.

Opposite, top: Coronation of King George VI, 1937. A party of children from the Windmill Lane area, photographed in Windmill Terrace — then a short cul-de-sac, now part of Delamare Road.

Opposite, bottom: Coronation of Queen Elizabeth II, 1953. A group of children from Cromwell Avenue and nearby streets.

Above: Queen Elizabeth the Queen Mother at Rochford's nurseries, 1959. With her are Thomas Rochford and Leonard Madsen, chairman of the Lea Valley Growers Association. Her Majesty also visited A. Stevens', E. Stevens' and Pollard's nurseries, and had tea in a marquee on Rochford's sports ground at Turnford. (Picture: Hertfordshire Mercury).

Opposite, top: Princess Margaret at Bishops' College. The College celebrated its golden jubilee in 1959 and the Princess was guest of honour. Here she crosses Churchgate for the Festival Service in St Mary's Church, accompanied by the Principal, John Trillo (left) and the Vicar of Cheshunt, Arthur Green (right).

Opposite, bottom: In the year of the Queen's Silver Jubilee, 1977, Princess Margaret came again. This time she visited Goffs School and watched a historical pageant. She also viewed an exhibition of local history organised by Jack Edwards (second right) and admired a model of the church built by Mark Gimson, Ralph Greenwell and Anthony Dobra. Also pictured are Mr E. Vale (a teacher) and Dr C.G. Hadley (Headmaster).

Above: This photo from Fishpool's own records is captioned "Our new 5-ton Dennis pantechnicon, 1932."

Below: Ernest Fishpool established his business north of its present site in 1899.   This advertisement of 1901 shows a typical Victorian interior.

Fishpool's original premises, from an advertising postcard of about 1905. Mr Fishpool stands at the door; at the side there is a two-horse pantechnicon. There would be some frenzied furniture shifting if it came on to rain.

SHOPS

Before car ownership made out-of-town shopping a viable proposition, most shopping was done on a day-to-day basis at the corner shop or in the local High Street. A major event was a shopping trip by bus or Green Line to Enfield Town or Oxford Street.

Above: Fishpool's store, with "40 large showrooms," decorated for the coronation in 1953. All the goods are now behind glass.

Opposite, top: Fishpool's present premises in about 1907, soon after they occupied them. Furniture is still displayed on the pavement, and a carpet hangs down from the roof at the right.

Opposite, bottom: O.S. Clarke's Waltham Cross Supply Stores, about 1910. This stood in High Street, Waltham Cross, opposite Park Lane, and went bankrupt in 1921. "Grand Butter" is advertised at 1s per pound, "Butter" at 10d. By a top floor window is a hoist for taking in deliveries.

Above: Metcalf's Emporium in Waltham New Town (Holdbrook North) at the time of the 1902 coronation. This shop did a lot of trade on the "never-never" ——"A Suit of Clothes for 1s a Week" ——"A Pair of Boots for 6d a Week." It prospered, and later was run by Mr H.C. Parker; it survived until the development of Holdbrook in the 1960s.

Below: Ripley the butcher in Turners Hill, premises still occupied by the same family business. In the doorway is Ernest Ripley with his son Leslie. The placards on the carcases are dated 1923 and say "Fed by the King." As they were sold at Slough Cattle Market they probably came from the royal estates at Windsor.

Nothing "on tick" here: King's Cash Stores in Crossbrook Street, near the Coach and Horses, in about 1912. Small shops like these, away from the main centres, catered for very small areas.

Above: Bakery at the Old Pond, next to the old Police Station, where the Tesco/Barclays building is now. Run by F.G. Gervais when this photo was taken in about 1960, many remember it as Ruffle's.

Opposite, top: C. & A. Blaxland's shop in Cheshunt High Street, 1935. Mr Tom Blaxland is at the shop door and his delivery van emerges from the yard. At this time Blaxland's were supplying the hotel at Theobalds Park.

Opposite, bottom: Interior of Blaxland's shop, 1935. Customers could sit on the wicker chairs, place their orders and have them delivered later in the day. The site was redeveloped in the late 1960s and is now occupied by the Gateway supermarket.

Above: Flamstead End Post Office and Stores, 1955. These buildings were opposite The Plough, where there is now a row of modern shops and flats. The Post Office was here for only a few years, having previously been in Hardwick's premises and moving later to Church Lane Newsagency. The garage was a smithy in the 1930s.

Opposite, top: A small "off-centre" shop in Goffs Lane below Goffs Oak village, 1955. This is a good example of the way shops drew attention to themselves by means of enamelled advertisements.

Opposite, bottom: Bullimore's, confectioners and tobacconists, on the northern point of the triangle at the Old Pond, 1955. To the left is a shoemaker's called "Bring 'em to George."

Above: The Queen Eleanor, north-west of Waltham Cross station bridge on what was the approach to a level crossing. The site is now occupied by a faceless office block. The message on this card, sent in 1906, says "Come and have a drop of gin, old dear. When are you coming to see us?"

Below: The Rose and Crown, Turners Hill, about 1910. Smith's milk cart offers alternative refreshment from its churn. The recently revived custom of decorating pubs with flowering plants was popular in Edwardian days.

The Britannia, Station Road, about 1950. Handy for Waltham Abbey residents alighting at Waltham Cross station.

PUBS

Like most towns, Cheshunt used to have many more inns and taverns than it does today. This was especially true of the main road, from the Middlesex boundary through to Turnford, because there was so much passing trade from medieval days onwards.

Right: This pen sketch shows the Britannia in about 1850 — the same building, with a flag pole even then.

Road side Inn near Waltham Station

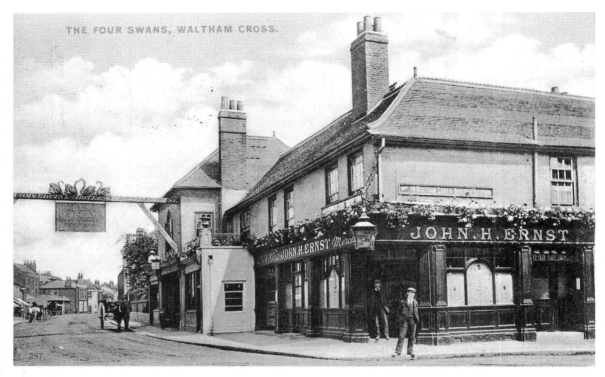

Above: The Four Swans, Waltham Cross. An early Charles Martin card, used in August 1904. As we saw earlier, this fine old building was demolished to make way for the shopping pavilion.

Below: Four Swans bill-head of about the same date - J. H. Ernst, proprietor. The date 1260 on the sign is a great exaggeration.

Fred McMullen, landlord of The Old Pond, photographed in 1953. Fred and his sister Blanche kept this house for very many years.

Above: The Old English Gentleman, Turners Hill, about 1938. This was built in 1898 on the site of an earlier pub which was owned by one George English in 1782. It still stands, with a modern extension.

Opposite, top: The Cricketers, College Road, on the south side of the triangle at the Old Pond. Christies were brewing at Hoddesdon from 1811 until they sold out to the Cannon Brewery of London in 1928.

Opposite, bottom: The Victoria, Turners Hill, just north of the almshouses. This old inn was rebuilt in about 1905. It is said that boys threw stones at the tin chimney; a direct hit brought down soot all over irate drinkers round the fireplace below.

Above: The Red Lion, on the west side of Cheshunt High Street, south of Brookfield Lane, photographed in about 1960. This fine timber-framed building was swept away in the wholesale clearance of the area a few years later.

Opposite, top: The Woolpack Tavern, Cheshunt High Street (opposite Cadmore Lane). This photo dates from before 1911, when the pub was rebuilt in its present form.

Opposite, bottom: The New River Arms. Now a Beefeater, this was built in 1936 as a road house for passing motorists on the Great Cambridge Road. The original sign, showing the arms of the New River Company, is now in Lowewood Museum.

The Jolly Bargeman on the canal towpath, east of Cheshunt station, in about 1890. Carefully posed to demonstrate a variety of sports. Long disused as a pub, the building was burnt down and demolished in 1983.

Above: The Crocodile, College Road: looking east, about 1905. Converted from two or three Victorian cottages; all were demolished in about 1980 for a new Crocodile set back from the road.

Below: The Green Dragon, Churchgate, opposite the church. A 16th century building with later additions and a 19th century facade, the justices met here in the 18th century. This view is about 1905.

Above: The Wheelwrights, Goffs Lane, 1959. This, the original pub, was on the south side of Goffs Lane and in the 1850s was owned by a wheelwright. A large new house now stands on the site, and a new Wheelwrights has arisen almost opposite.

Opposite, top: The Prince of Wales at the corner of Burton Lane and St James' Road, Goffs Oak. Built in late Victorian days in what was then a remote spot; there were not even any nurseries around it at that time. This photo about 1928.

Opposite, bottom: The Rising Sun, Hammond Street, about 1905. Another late Victorian pub serving a very small scattered population of cottagers. But this was the hey-day of the bicycle; perhaps it catered for trippers.

Prince of Wales Inn, Goffs Oak.

The "Rising Sun" Hotel, Goffs Oak.

William Cecil, Lord Burghley (National Portrait Gallery)

CHESHUNT PEOPLE

William Cecil, Lord Burghley, Lord Treasurer to Queen Elizabeth I, bought Theobalds in 1563 and built the huge house, where he entertained the queen on fourteen occasions up to his death in 1598. He spent much time at Theobalds, a convenient country retreat from court affairs.

King James I visited Theobalds in 1603 when travelling from Edinburgh to London on his accession. Four years later he persuaded Robert Cecil to take Hatfield in exchange for Theobalds, where the king enjoyed hunting and entertaining foreign rulers and statesmen. King James died here in 1625.

Opposite, top: John Tillotson, Archbishop of Canterbury 1691-94, was curate of Cheshunt under Thomas Hackett, vicar, from 1661 to 1663. This was his first parochial post, and he lived with Sir Thomas Dacres at Cheshunt Great House. In later years he occasionally rented the Great House as a summer residence. (National Portrait Gallery).

Opposite, bottom: Self-portrait of James Ward, painter of animals and Royal Academician, who lived at Roundcroft in Park Lane, Cheshunt, for the last thirty years of his life. He died there in 1859 at the age of 90. The Tate Gallery put on an exhibition of his work in 1960. (National Portrait Gallery).

Above: Anthony Trollope, novelist and Post Office official, lived at Waltham House from 1859 to 1871 while at the height of his literary powers. Such artistic friends as Thackeray and Millais visited him here.

Opposite, top: Mr Morgan of Eleanor Road was a postman at Waltham Cross. Here he poses with a bundle of letters in his hand and three long-service bars on his breast.

Opposite, bottom: Alexis Doxat, V.C. The son of E.T. Doxat of Woodgreen Park, Silver Street, Alec Doxat won his award in South Africa in 1900 by riding under heavy Boer fire to pick up a comrade whose horse had been shot under him. Doxat died at Cambridge in 1942.

Above: F.G. Debenham and his wife had two sons and five daughters. This picture of about 1900 shows, left to right, Mary, Grace (later Mrs John Wanklyn), Amy, Phillis, and Christina. Mrs Wanklyn died young, but the four unmarried sisters lived on at Cheshunt Park for many years; Phillis, the youngest, died aged 91 in 1968.

Left: Frank Gissing Debenham (1832-1912). As a prosperous young estate agent in the City Mr Debenham took a lease of Cheshunt Park in 1865 and lived there until his death. He was educated at Bruce Castle School under Arthur Hill, Sir Rowland Hill's brother. While at Cheshunt Park he did much local charitable work, but declined municipal and county appointments.

Above: Sir Henry Bruce Meux and his wife Lady Valerie (then still plain Mr and Mrs Meux) on holiday in Scotland in 1880. H.B. Meux succeeded to the baronetcy in 1883 and the couple took up residence in Theobalds Park in 1885.

Above: Four generations in the female line: a fine costume piece of 1898. On the left is Mrs Walklate, whose husband was a draper in what are now Fishpool's premises. Seated is her mother, Mrs Craske. On the right is Mrs Lily Tingle, nee Walklate, holding her baby daughter Madge — who later became Mrs Ernest Rochford of Turnford.

Opposite, top: A group of local nurserymen: many well-remembered names here. A cartoonist's impression of the Lea Valley Growers Association Executive Dinner, February 1949.

Opposite, bottom: George Jennings, chauffeur to Thomas Rochford, in his employer's 12 h.p. Rover in Brookfield Lane, 1915. Jennings wore a dark green uniform and the car's radiator and lamps were silver plated.

RYAN F. MEERING

P. J. BUTTERFIELD

L. J. CLAPHAM   N. G. SHOULTS   L. C. MADSEN   E. STEVENS   BERNARD ROCHFORD, O.B.E., J.P., Y.M.H.   E. C. GALLOWAY   J. P. ROCHFORD, Jr., Y.M.H.   A. ALBURY POLLARD, J.P.   P. M. CHRISTENSEN
                                                                          Chairman.   *President.*

L. A. J. HAKANSSON

R. A. F. FAIRHURST   L. A. WILTON   R. E. FOURACRES   C. D. CHAPMAN   HORACE DREW,   G. B. POLLARD   F. HANCE   LT-COL. J. LEACH   A. B. STEVENS
                                                                          Secretary.

Left: F.H. Rudling as "Charley's Aunt," about 1925. Mr Rudling joined the staff of Dewhurst School in about 1908 and became its Headmaster in 1938. Because of the war he carried on beyond retirement age, resigning his post in September 1945. He died in 1961 aged 82.

Opposite, top: Mr and Mrs Percy Hargreaves in their garden at Whit Hern, about 1950. Mr Hargreaves was one of four brothers all prominent in the London marine insurance market, and was Chairman of Lloyd's of London in 1931. He was born in Cheshunt and lived at Whit Hern for about 20 years until his death in 1955 aged 87.

Oposite, bottom: Flamstead End Women's Institute members in costume for a play in the 1950s. Left to right: Mrs Godden, Mrs Chaplin, Mrs Stevens, Mrs Ells. Picture taken at Mrs Godden's home, no. 17 Churchgate.

Above: A.F. Saunders, "window cleaner & carpet beater, 3 College Rd, Cheshunt. Insured at own risk." Mr Saunders' address was between the Old Pond pub and the Central Cinema. This picture about 1930.

Below: Fred Barratt delivering greengroceries in Cromwell Avenue, about 1953, with his young helper Andrew Ransome. Barratt's shop in Turners Hill was where Lynton Parade is now.

Above: After a confirmation service at St Clement's, Turnford, in 1957, with the Bishop of Bedford (Campbell MacInnes). Back row, first left: Mr A.T. Foord; first right: Dr T.R. Trounce; third right: the Revd John Hasted (priest in charge). Third from right, front row, Michael Dobbs, author of "House of Cards" and "To Play the King," and deputy chairman of the Conservative Party.

Below: After Mass at St Joseph's Church, 1977: Cardinal Basil Hume greets members of the congregation (Picture: Carleton Photographic)

Index